SCIENCE BEHIND THE COLORS
FRILLED LIZARDS

by Alicia Z. Klepeis

Ideas for Parents and Teachers

Pogo Books let children practice reading informational text while introducing them to nonfiction features such as headings, labels, sidebars, maps, and diagrams, as well as a table of contents, glossary, and index.

Carefully leveled text with a strong photo match offers early fluent readers the support they need to succeed.

Before Reading

- "Walk" through the book and point out the various nonfiction features. Ask the student what purpose each feature serves.
- Look at the glossary together. Read and discuss the words.

Read the Book

- Have the child read the book independently.
- Invite him or her to list questions that arise from reading.

After Reading

- Discuss the child's questions. Talk about how he or she might find answers to those questions.
- Prompt the child to think more. Ask: Frilled lizards scare predators with their colorful frills. Do you know any other animals that can do something like this?

Pogo Books are published by Jump!
5357 Penn Avenue South
Minneapolis, MN 55419
www.jumplibrary.com

Library of Congress Cataloging-in-Publication Data

Names: Klepeis, Alicia, 1971- author.
Title: Frilled lizards / by Alicia Z. Klepeis.
Description: Minneapolis, MN: Jump!, Inc., [2022]
Series: Science behind the colors | Includes index.
Audience: Ages 7-10
Identifiers: LCCN 2021032456 (print)
LCCN 2021032457 (ebook)
ISBN 9781636903736 (hardcover)
ISBN 9781636903743 (paperback)
ISBN 9781636903750 (ebook)
Subjects: LCSH: Frilled lizard—Juvenile literature.
Frilled lizard—Color—Juvenile literature.
Classification: LCC QL666.L223 K58 2022 (print)
LCC QL666.L223 (ebook) | DDC 597/.61—dc23
LC record available at https://lccn.loc.gov/2021032456
LC ebook record available at
https://lccn.loc.gov/2021032457

Editor: Eliza Leahy
Designer: Emma Bersie

Photo Credits: DWI YULIANTO/Shutterstock, cover, 18-19; PetlinDmitry/Shutterstock, 1; GlobalP/iStock, 3; Ken Griffiths/Shutterstock, 4, 8-9, 17; blickwinkel/Alamy, 5; Bildagentur Zoonar GmbH/Shutterstock, 6-7; Auscape International Pty Ltd/Alamy, 10-11; Wayan Sumatika/Dreamstime, 12; Matt Cornish/Shutterstock, 13, 20-21; Kurit afshen/Shutterstock, 14-15 (foreground), 16; Ecopix/Shutterstock, 14-15 (background); Eric Isselee/Shutterstock, 23.

Printed in the United States of America at Corporate Graphics in North Mankato, Minnesota.

TABLE OF CONTENTS

CHAPTER 1

FROM DULL TO BRIGHT

A frilled lizard rests on a branch. This **reptile** is hard to see. Its **scales** are dark brown to light gray. This **camouflage** helps it hide.

scales

Frilled lizards live in Australia and New Guinea. Many live in forests. They spend most of their time in trees. But they will go to the ground to hunt. They are **carnivores**. They mostly eat insects.

insect

frill

These lizards are named for the **frills** around their necks. A lizard's frill is a loose flap of skin. When it is folded up, its color looks dull.

But if a lizard feels **threatened**, it will **flex** its throat muscles. This makes the frill pop up! Suddenly, the lizard looks bigger. We see its bright colors.

This can happen when a **predator** gets close. Snakes and birds hunt frilled lizards.

DID YOU KNOW?

Frilled lizards have colorful mouths and tongues, too! They are pink or yellow.

frill

What if the frill doesn't scare the predator? Frilled lizards are good runners! They can run more than nine miles (14 kilometers) per hour. They often run to trees to hide.

DID YOU KNOW?

Frilled lizards are also called bicycle lizards. Why? When they run, their legs move like they are pedaling bicycles.

CHAPTER 2

FLASHY FRILLS

How do frilled lizards get their colors? Some come from **pigments** their bodies make. Others come from pigments in the food they eat.

Not all frills are the same color. Lizards with red or orange frills have more pigments in their skin. These may come from their food or their **genes**.

Frill color also depends on where a lizard lives. One in western Australia might have a red frill. One in northeastern Australia might have a yellow or white frill. Why? Scientists believe the food they eat plays a part. Another idea is that different colors stand out more in different **environments**.

TAKE A LOOK!

How are frill colors different across Australia? Take a look!

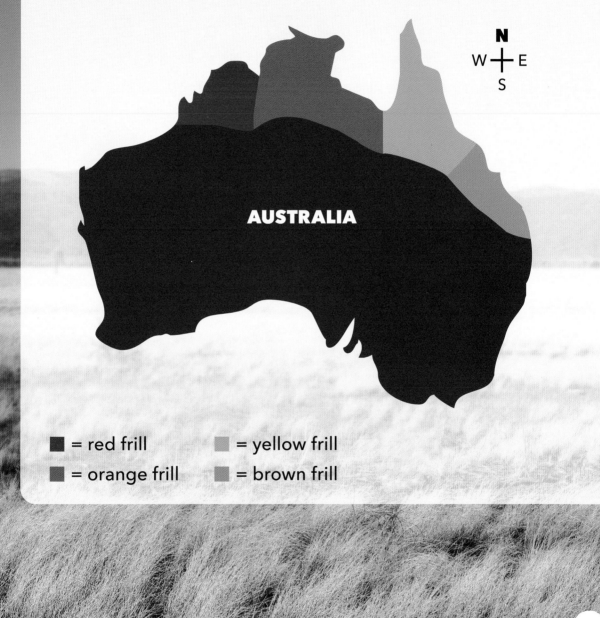

N
W + E
S

AUSTRALIA

■ = red frill   ■ = yellow frill
■ = orange frill   ■ = brown frill

CHAPTER 3

FIGHTING WITH FRILLS

Young frilled lizards are gray.
This helps them hide.
They stay safe in trees.

They develop their bright colors as **juveniles**. By age one and a half, they have bright frills.

Both males and females have bright frills. Males use theirs to fight. They defend their **territories**. The bright colors tell others to stay away!

These lizards are famous for their frills. Their bright colors warn off danger. They may also help them find **mates**. Would you like to see one?

DID YOU KNOW?

The brighter the frill, the healthier the lizard. A colorful frill can show that a lizard is good at finding food.

TRY THIS!

SPREADING PIGMENTS

Frilled lizards get their colors from pigments. See how pigments spread in this fun activity!

What You Need:
- scissors
- white coffee filter
- black marker
- ruler
- mug
- water

1. Cut out a circle from the coffee filter. The circle should be about the size of your hand when your fingers are spread out.

2. Use a black marker and a ruler to draw a thick line about 1 inch (2.5 centimeters) above the bottom of the circle.

3. Pour a small amount of water into the mug. It should just cover the bottom of the mug.

4. Curl the circle into the mug. The bottom of the circle should be in the water. The line you drew should be above the surface of the water.

5. Watch the water flow up the coffee filter. What happens when the water touches the black line? Leave the filter in the water until colors go all the way up the mug. What colors do you see?

camouflage: A disguise or natural coloring that allows animals to hide by making them look like their surroundings.

carnivores: Animals that eat meat.

environments: The natural surroundings of living things.

flex: To tighten a muscle.

frills: Leathery ruffs of skin located around the necks of frilled lizards.

genes: Parts of living things that are passed from parents to offspring and determine how one looks and grows.

juveniles: Young animals.

mates: The breeding partners of a pair of animals.

pigments: Substances that give color to something.

predator: An animal that hunts other animals for food.

reptile: A cold-blooded animal that crawls across the ground or creeps on short legs and usually reproduces by laying eggs.

scales: The thin, flat, overlapping pieces of hard skin that cover the bodies of reptiles and fish.

territories: Areas of land that animals claim and defend.

threatened: In danger.

INDEX

TO LEARN MORE

Finding more information is as easy as 1, 2, 3.

1 Go to www.factsurfer.com

2 Enter "frilledlizards" into the search box.

3 Choose your book to see a list of websites.

FACT SURFER